KV-373-787

Tormentil

Tormentil

Ian Humphreys

Nine
Arches
Press

Tormentil
Ian Humphreys

ISBN: 978-1913437787
eISBN: 978-1913437794

Copyright © Ian Humphreys, 2023.

Cover artwork: Design by Jane Commane. Tormentil pictured in an antique illustration of medicinal and herbal plants, published in 1892 in *Medicinal Plants of Russia*. Scan by Ivan Burmistrov.

All rights reserved. No part of this work may be reproduced, stored or transmitted in any form or by any means, graphic, electronic, recorded or mechanical, without the prior written permission of the publisher.

Ian Humphreys has asserted his right under Section 77 of the Copyright, Designs and Patents Act 1988 to be identified as the author of this work.

First published September 2023 by:

Nine Arches Press
Unit 14, Sir Frank Whittle Business Centre,
Great Central Way, Rugby.
CV21 3XH
United Kingdom

www.ninearchespress.com

Printed on recycled paper in the United Kingdom
by Imprint Digital.

Nine Arches Press is supported using public funding
by Arts Council England.

for Mum

Contents

Tormentil

I can't face the big stuff
so I comb the moors
for a tiny yellow flower,
treasured in wartime
for healing wounds.
Some named it Bloodroot
or Flesh and Blood,
others, Shepherd's Knot.
Up here, gold thread
creeps through boggy
peatland grass. Splashes
of sun under a dark sky.

Earthworm on tarmac

O silent concertina:
one mouth, five hearts,
one arsehole.
Dirt pearls
cast in your wake.
How did you get here
needled
by the furious sun?
Half an hour ago,
soft sanctuary.
The drag
of home
through your body.
I could pick you up,
flick you
onto the grass verge.
I could leave you
frying on the kerb,
plump & sausage-pink.
The magpie
would thank me
& that curious child,
his scalpel
fingernails.
Can you eat pain
earthworm?
Do you swallow
buried mistakes?
You, who ploughs

the muck at our feet,
stirs the soup
of forests past.
Earthworm,
are you worth
bending for?
Kneeling for?

the grasshopper warbler's song

the singing will never be done
 – Siegfried Sassoon

rising and dipping
cool seeds of springtime
hidden in the long grass
notes balanced
on swaying stems
mirroring
the viola flow
        of bristled leg against wing
rising and dipping
no melody
        just
        air decanted
        just
    how light through cloud might sound
following footsteps like green shadows
rising and dipping
rousing as a chorus
softer than feather moss

and the grass and the trees and the sky

First signs

After I post the snowdrops photo,
a friend opens up: *I could use some hope x*

Seems everyone's hurting and down with cold
and your Alzheimer's has stopped you cooking.

You no longer know saffron from salt,
can't quite appraise the depth of blue glazed

serving bowls or savour late morning light
sprinkled over the church roof. And when I think of it,

I don't remember the last time your clay pot sputtered
and clunked on the stove. The communion

of rice, Chinese sausage and shiitake mushrooms
filling the house with a blessing.

Lady Luck

You'd never seen snow   it slid through your fingers like rice flour
        You missed your flat   on Prince Edward Road
    Mong Kok's leaning towers   of dim sum baskets
In Hythe   boiled-cabbage streets steamed with winter breath
    Under a cold tin sink   your carved camphorwood chest
        cradled memories in padded brocade   You developed
cravings for pickled sea snails   bought a tub every day
    Gran worried   baby would be born   with whelk-shaped ears
        On the sea-front   heads turned like waltzers
they admired your blue-black hair   they gave you extra chips
        Sometimes   they touched you for luck

Bad egg

When Hobbes came for tea
you made Scotch egg and salad.
I wanted English

egg and chips.
But at least it wasn't Macanese Minchee
or Bafassa or Lup Lup.

To draw his gawp from your
clacking chopsticks
I passed him the tomato sauce.

Do you know the Chinese
invented ketchup? you said.
It's Heinz, I muttered, skewering my food.

Crispy gold-crumb crust.
A whisper of steam. Sweet pink meat.
Then a gentle kick

of chilli. How quickly Hobbes drained
his tumbler of orange squash. He complained
later the egg was so spicy

his lips were burning.
His lips were burning
until the next day when I saw him sniggering

with Buller in chemistry.
Buller, who smoked No. 6 and stank
of bacon butties.

Wasp in a jam jar

A sticky August afternoon. Our neat street
swoons in the heatwave. The smell of burning
eggs spirals from a forgotten frying pan. Or
was it the fresh-laid tarmac sweating chemicals
yards from my bedroom. Or the forbidden boys
shirtless in glue-on scowls, torching a blown tyre
in the precinct. Later I watched them necking
cider on the library steps, dead-legging, flicking
through a top-shelf glossy. Each flare of laughter
stung. Dad got angry when he found out
they'd planted palm prints in the soft tar.
I couldn't tell him it was me. Feeling my way
into the dark, marking the road out of there.

Pansies

The Wild Pansy is found on disturbed
ground. They flower once, seed and die off.
Also known as Tickle-my-fancy.

– *Pansies Quarterly* (Autumn Issue, 1971)

I still adore them even though
we really shouldn't – the old guard
from the sixties and seventies. Those
confirmed bachelors who played fey.
Sharpened pennies tossed to the crowd
from pursed lips. Laugh at me, Duckie,
not with me. Camp compliance
trowelled thick as luvvie slap. Dick,
Frankie, Larry, Charles, Mr Humphries,
Kenneth's *What's the bloody point?*
Cilla's confidante upstairs at The Black Cap
who didn't like Pride, preferred sex
when it was illegal. *I dunno, hun,*
it just felt dirty, thrilling back then.

Hak gwai

As my great aunt in Hong Kong lay dying
the ward nurse quizzed her daughter
How is this woman related to you?
She's my mother, Pam replied.
No, I mean, who is she really?
I told you, she's my mother. *She can't be*
the ward nurse insisted. *You're Chinese.*
She's black.

After my cousin told this story, I asked
if the nurse had used hak gwai
– black devil in Cantonese.
It was a name people offered my own mother
when she was a child as though handing her
a dried salted plum. Mum emigrated at twenty
and learned the English
rarely said such things to your face.

Walltown

They knew how to build walls in these parts. Dry stone walls.
Two-foot thick in places. Gritstone. Grey or rain-cloud black.
Stacked for purpose. Sheep peer through the cracks.
Private. Today many have toppled into disrepair.
Forgotten. Where to find a waller skilled in the old ways?
They're rarer than foxes round here now. Just last week
in a walled-off field, I found four foxes laid out, side by side.
No marks on their pelts, no bullet wounds. Flames for tails.
Two adults, two cubs. Trim and tidy. A family of day-trippers
enjoying a nap in the sun. The day was still and steep like
the terraces that fortress the valley and tops. Over-dwellings.
Under-dwellings. Walls of eyes. Keep Out. The biggest wall
stalks Keighley Road. Thirty feet high. Its crevices bursting
with moss, ferns, jittery wrens. Walls that size hold back
rivers, stop hillsides moving in on us. Blood-rooted.
Shadow walls lay low, ivy-cloaked in ancient woodland.
Carcasses of mills and tumbledown crone-houses. What do they
hold back? I'm back in that pub where they uncovered
a mummified cat behind the fireplace. They'd brick them up,
dead or alive, to thwart evil spirits from entering the home.
Private. Keep Out. I saw a horse kick down a section of wall once
before sniffing the fallen stones. It whinnied and stared
at the next field then took a step back, settling on staying put.

Petrified

Our cherry tree is bleeding
golden sap from an open wound.
The secretion glows like hot-glass,
slowly hardening at its core.
A chequered hoverfly lands close,
lingers in stasis. Is it contemplating
a step towards immortality?
Minutes creep by. I could stay here
all day or for eighty million years
trapped by indecision. I will
phone the hospital. But first,
I must dead-head the roses. That's me,
slipping back into morning's bright
stickiness, sweat beading brow.

Scrimshander

If I could carve the truth into my bones,
I would show you the ship that beached me,
clubbed me, bled the oil from my fire.
I would show how people take treasure
from the seas, hurl curses at the hurricane.
One message in a billion plastic bottles.
Because bones pay no heed to time,
I would raise the Atlantic above cliffs, hang
human skeletons from a domed glass sky,
to be eyed by curious gulls. I'd show cities burning
underwater. And my magnum opus?
Two long black fins, whittled and inked
along the smile of a rib bone,
cutting through the North Sea for home.

The other lot

have hearts of anthracite
we scuff with pick axes
in candle-ruddy tunnels. They drive cars.
The other lot drink from flutes – flutes! –
spread-eagled on grand pianos,
address the room in timpani rumbles.
They laugh at our gods. The other lot
treat pain with paper pills,
send their Chihuahuas to the very
best schools. If you ask the other lot
for a hand up, you'll get a platinum slap
or a crocodile boot. Some say not all
the other lot are as bad as that lot
but those people are secretly the other lot.
They wear spun history. They fundraise,
build monuments, twist language
to keep our lot in our moleholes.
They mine darker pits to hurl us into.
                    Everyone knows they're not like us.
                        Their hands are gigantic sponges,
            their brains hard-wired with tales of woe.
                    The other lot haul around grey lungs
                    and bellies scarred with palm oil.
        They feed their narwhals chicken nuggets.
        All day long, they slump on snorebags
                        blinking at the flickering sky.
                    Their men covet our cars – and,
            and on Fridays, lacerate each other
                    with broken vinegar bottles.

What they really need is a shortsharpshake
to get their stopped clocks ticking.
Our lot have little in common
with that god-spooked rabble.
They speak in peculiar syntaxes,
often bandage themselves in silences
longer than our history. My heart weeps
rubies for them, but seriously, that lot.

On spilling a jug of Mai Tai plus half a pale ale over the new marketing director's lap during her welcome drinks

In a Huddersfield beer garden,
the A-frame picnic table wobbles
     when I wish myself tiny.

Shazam! I'm an earwig –
Forficula auricularia – skittering from
     the brass-rimmed parasol hole

onto a sky-blue dish of scampi
flavour fries. Boss
     knuckles half of them.

Crunch! I reincarnate
as a midge – sandwiched
     between a double-ginned priest

and a wilting plastic palm.
I jitterbug at dusk with my new
     blood-sucking colleagues,

fizz-bomb a woman
burping Prosecco. *Splat!*
     Karma spits me back as

a single skin cell on the
snippy waiter's sun-flared neck.
    I dandruff down

to lightly season
our Head of HR's warm pear cider.
    Cheers! I'm a virus now,

entombed inside a complex
mucus molecule that surfs
    a vaping hipster's sneeze until

I'm washed-up on a salt dune
of jumbo peanuts, shadowed
    once again by the greedy hand

of Boss.

desire

I wait for my photo at a photo booth, and out comes someone else's face
 - Marion, the trapeze artist, *Wings of Desire*

some mornings I audit myself
in the bathroom mirror and think
        you got this far
twenty years I worked those offices
            pretending
to get high from line after line
of superlatives and tired puns
                        keyboard kingpin
till one day someone said
we need to winkle out the fascination
from this low-grade tinned tuna

        a fissure

            that night
the owl flew from my sleep
into a moon-startled room
she clung to the curtain ruffles
        her familiar face white with rage
how dare I disturb
            such beautiful mechanics

Liberté

Sue from Crewe
taught me how to fry an egg in a chip pan.
Why waste time and electricity
juggling two pots? Sue was green
when green was unfashionable.
Saves on washing-up liquid too. I sweated
that a dropped watery egg might ignite
the bubbling lard and one day
it did. In a heartbeat

                         Sue snatched
our dinner from the hob, strode
into the back garden and held the blaze
at arm's length – ciggie firm between lips.
Quick, buggerlugs, fetch me a wrung-out
wet tea towel and I'll smother the bastard.

Firecrest

Like a small cinder
it bursts
from the trees.

Feathered crown
yellow
as the waspy gorse

by the dried up
moorland pool.
Yellow

as the lichen
sequinning
a stone burial mound.

Yellow
as the wings
of goldfinches

their fleeting charm
and the tormentil
that binds

hill to vale.
Those frail stars
magnified

by a pitched
lemonade bottle.
And every yellow

eclipsed
by the sun.
She scours the thicket

for a wick.
Glories
in her golden children

marching
through the parched
yellowing grass.

There's a walrus on my windscreen

and my wipers can't wipe it off, thud-up
against the bristle-blubber-blood of it. It
came here from Greenland – diggerscooped
from Baffin Bay by that crazy polar vortex
then re-routed to a snowblitz above my
Hummer. David blames it all on global
whatsit. Critically, he says, we're past the
critical point. Yesterday, a musk ox totalled
the Guptas' Land Cruiser and
Mrs Tripp found three thirds of
an arctic fox sprawled across her back yard –
sliced like salad egg by the power lines.
Her Siberian larch decking

                                won't recover.
Why take the grandkids to the zoo?
Every week, doorstep trophies flung
from far lands – pink flamingos
stinking up the hydrotherapy hot tub,
lines of armadillos bowling
down the alley through the bins. I
once found a desiccated hand
while bleaching the gutters. Candice swore
it was orangutan but to me it felt
human: palm open, fingers cupped, empty.

The wood pigeon's song

The world bleeds, Betty
The world bleeds, Betty
The world bleeds, Betty
The world

rubber pup at the Queer Rights in Chechnya rally

led from your en suite kennel   in Hale Barns
to Sackville Gardens   where a radical
trans feminist   distributes condoms and
cupcakes   where a charm of cider-rouged lads
greets the cute refugee   from Nigeria as if
Miss Grace Jones Herself   commands
the stage   where the statue of Alan Turing sits
and watches the world go
backwards   good boy good boy   you applaud
with clenched latex paws   chew on
those dark places   those countries
where desire is muzzled   men caged   put down
for the chase   bad boy bad boy
you don't whimper or beg   just wag your
placard   *I choose   who treats me like an animal*

Babysitting in Ho Man Tin

I walk into my bachelor pad and see an ape
hanging from the ceiling light, swinging
round and round with a nappy on his head.
He shrieks and leaps into my arms. For seven days,
this month-old Cambodian gibbon, unshackled
from the black market, adopts me as his city mother.

He eats only grapes, play-bites the kitten's paws.
At night, his liana limbs entwine my neck.
Each breath, a swallowtail flutter. Disposable
wipes keep him dry and I soothe chafed legs
with palm oil lotion. Months after he's rehomed,
I crazydream of giant safety-pins and a baby

dangling from the jungle canopy, his real mother
reaching out, unable to touch her child. He turns to her
but his face is my face. Our umbilical cord snakes
into the red gape of a pitcher plant. In a blink,
I'm swaddled in cotton, pram, England – awakening
under an ocean of sky. Looking up in wonder.

Of course, I don't mind

It's just I feel sad you'll never have children.

Remote

Some memories you lost
down the back of the sofa
while watching repeats

of Midsomer Murders, Midsomer Murders.
Others you kept safe,
stacked in Tupperware

on the kitchen counter.
Dates, chocolate digestives,
moon cakes, melon seeds

and babies
in every colour of the test card.
Sweet, squidgy, powdered.

The sign language of trees

A pink-dreadlocked woman
strimming the allotment stops
to adjust the bra strap on her scarecrow.
That's when the beech tree

emits a warning. The V of its bulk
slow-splinters and its mast crashes
on the old boundary wall.
As the bough gives way it leaves a void

scattering sovereigns of light
across the pond.
A top-stone tumbles into raspberries.
Mutiny of sparrows.

In the certainty of afternoon
one pale, severed limb
points towards the road to Pecket Well.
I turn to look, shield my eyes.

When trees burn

After Philip Larkin

The blackthorn blazes white in bloom
before its spirit fades to leaf.
Spring's beacon shines, disowning grief
disarming winter's last-gasp gloom.

It seems to sing out start afresh
all things must change. An assurance
of brighter days, the heady dance
of bees, the modest fruit's dark flesh.

Punch and Judy on the West Yorkshire Moors

Last month it was beavers in the Cairngorms and now Punch and Judy have been spotted above Hebden Bridge. Free from the puppet master. Free from the fist. Punch is a new man, no kazoo cackle, no whacking stick. He gathers a lemon love posy for Judy. Buttercup,

tormentil, broom. She whittles arrows from blackthorn. *We've meadow pipit for supper, Mr Punch.* Later, he'll weep vinegar and salt as his wife plucks, guts and cooks the bird over a peat fire. He still sports a jaunty hat while Judy's fashioned her maid's cap into a catapult sling. *I feel closer to God up here*, says Punch. *I don't need no man*

putting words in my mouth, says Judy. Empty inside, they ghost-float across the tops, flapping in the wind through burnt heather and half-blown cotton-grass. Free from the puppet master. Free from the fist. Free from hordes of screaming kids, candyfloss-clammy paws. Punch thinks his wife is searching for their baby but she's foraging.

He made me do it, Judy! She gathers armful after armful of dried grasses and moss, stuffs the gap left by the loss of that cold hand. Full now, and bent by thirst over a moorland pond, Judy catches sight of a bright red sea anemone billowing below. It's just her unpinned hair shimmering on the water's tension. The mirror kaleidoscopes into the face of crouching man, skeleton, armed police officer, and fixes on grinning crocodile. The beast surfaces. *Is this really the way to do it, madam?*

Free from the puppet master. Free from the fist, Judy replies, reaching for her bow and arrow.

love hurts

punched me in the gut one time   love
told me   I wasn't good enough
just go   love didn't care   waste of space
no one else would have me anyway   loser
love said   better not go crying to anyone
who would believe me   no friends
and every weekend   can't go out like that
gagging for it   a laughing stock
stole the wind from me yesterday   love did
threw a glass across the room   then me
but love was sorry   I can't leave   swore
it won't happen again   swore on my life
and don't you know when you abandon love
like smoke abandons fire   or down on its knees
in a flooded underpass   come dawn
back love strides   whistling your song
wearing your skin   threatening
to kick in the door   no need love   it's open

Rope-grown mussels

That first morning
by the docks
we hardly spoke to each other.
I remember
the laughing fisherman.
How we helped
unload his harvest.
Eight overfull
washing-up bowls
dowsed and clinking
like broken crockery.
He called the farms
high-rise living
for shellfish.
They prefer it
to the seabed, he said.
Grow twice as big.
No predators, see.
We plunged in wrist deep
appalled
by the slipperiness.
Back at the house
I found a sword-shaped
letter opener
in a hinged tin box
and scraped off
barnacles
from the shiny
black molluscs.
Shallots. Chopped parsley.

A good bottle.
Striking lucky
with the last Cook's Match.
Pressing our fingers
against half-closed lips
to gently prise open
mouth
after wine-warmed mouth.
And inside each one
a tongue   plump
with sweetness and salt.

Nomi

The world hushed to white
the attosecond
your geisha pout blossomed
into song.
I picture you static on stage like a rare creature
preserved in formaldehyde, corseted
in spray-on spacesuit, trussed
and buckled, camber spine
a mast
for your see-through plastic cape.
You look stunned,
walloped by the lights,
red lips bloodless
under a twice-widowed peak.
With strange grace
your marionette hands lift in brittle surrender.
You were flummoxed by our world
right to the end.
Each night you'd scan the audience, unblinking,
knowing there was something out there,
waiting. I watched from the wings
the day the alien crackle
called you back.
As you clung to that final note, I prayed
it would last forever. But your kind
never sticks around.
Machine sounds whirred and
slowly you stepped back,
losing yourself
in a cold hymn,
a cough of dry ice.

Grey matter

You grease the pole holding
the bird feeder with cooking oil.

Now the big fat grey squirrel
can't reach the big fat white balls
of protein-loaded lard.

You watch him climb up, slide
down, climb up, slide down

pistoning while sparrows bicker
over their change in fortune.

You know you've done the right thing.
He just seems so put out
at his sudden loss of privilege.

Bushytailed boss man,
waiting for crumbs from the table.

Paucity

It's been a weak year for poetry　　　By which I mean
woke　　　It's been a dreadful
year for puppetry　　　Hardly anyone
I know　　　is pulling the strings
I suppose it's been　　　a so-so year for pedantry –
that's not literature　　　it's shouting!
Hasn't it been a terrible year　　　for pottery?
The bowl I made　　　back in the day
isn't half full of cherries　　　It's been a cool kind
of year for polarity　　　We polar bears seem to be
a dying breed　　　And what are all these
penguins doing here in the Arctic?　　　It's been
a poor year for potpourri　　　By that I mean
I'm not smelling of roses　　　It's been a slum year
for property　　　These rogue landlords
are scooping up　　　all the best contracts
Rotten year for pastry　　　Should've used my recipe
Sod's law, it's been a bona year　　　for Polari
If I was a neurodivergent　　　transitioning rent boy
I'd win the Forward Prize　　　Ghastly
year for pepperoni　　　What's wrong with
traditional toppings?　　　Tofu on a pizza?
It's been a slim year for poetry　　　By which I mean
it's been a slam year for poetry　　　By that I mean
I love their energy but　　　we're not on the same page

Whose story?

When I was a boy, my mum would tell me the tale of her great-grandfather: *The First Black Man to Ride a Horse in Hong Kong*. He was from Mozambique – a lone soldier who rode up and down Pottinger Street as if leading a military procession. He was decorated. This was back in the 1880s. Children flung open the shutters of pastel-stained shophouses to stare and point. As he trotted past, amahs threw buckets of laundry slops in his wake, washing away the sin. Men spat. *Hak Gwai*. Only white people were meant to take the air up on the hill (in later years, the Chinese were forbidden to live there), so my great-great-grandfather navigated the muggy lowlands, silent and straight-backed on his Arabian steed. He thought he might make friends with the Chinese, but they had found someone they could look down on. *Even though he drips with medals,* the elders said, *you can bet his heart is blacker than his skin.* Or perhaps their words had been sweetened that day by lychees and longans: *This foreigner is a warrior like Yasuke – the legendary Black Sumarai. We must treat him with respect.* Nobody knows where he met my great-great-grandmother, or how they eloped to Macau. To be honest, no one knows very much at all. I've dreamt up most of this story because my people's history is spun on whispers. And that one curious image of *The First Black Man to Ride a Horse in Hong Kong.* It's awful to admit, but things might be easier if my great-great-grandfather had been *The First White Man to Ride a Horse in Hong Kong.* At least then we'd have some answers, official documents of his life gathering dust in a museum. And, of course, a fine statue to commemorate the occasion. Man and horse. On a pedestal.

Refrain

There's a bird over there
famous for its song.
People have come from
as far as Cheshire
to hear its haunting mating call.
It arrived from South Africa
on Wednesday morning and
by teatime the local Airbnbs
had doubled their prices.
Someone brought
their grandmother along yesterday.
I can't hear anything, she said.
It isn't singing yet, Gran. Have a cheese string.
We've been here two days now
still nothing.
Phones have died. Flasks have cooled.
Shoulders frozen.
The town paper ran a piece
on a smiling dog instead.
What on earth is wrong with the thing?
Look at it
sitting there on that branch
being quiet.

Discarded wardrobe on Deansgate

I stepped inside when no-one was looking,
it was half full of magic and half full of moths.
The clothes had been chomped off my back
by the time I reached the secret door
to another world. Annoyingly, it was locked
and spray-painted: NO ENTRY. Naked,
except for a uniform layer of dust,
I froze, far too embarrassed to step out
onto the pavement again. I survived
on mothballs which I sucked like gobstoppers,
and gobstoppers I found glued inside
the pockets of small duffle coats,
school blazers and shiny biker jackets.
The soft babble of pedestrians kept me alive,
old River Dene rolling about her business.
By the fourth day, I started to wonder
how long I could last in there now all the skins
from my past were empty. That's when
I sensed someone standing next to me
in the dark, someone who wasn't frightened.

Wrong uns

The certainty saved me.
Certainly.
Somehow, I knew
from a very early age
that they were all wrong.
And I was alright.

Like a record, baby

Last night, a boy told me
he'd travelled over 4,000 miles
to dance at Queens Court
and that if he spun fast enough
really fast
he could make the world rotate
a little quicker
days glimmer that bit sooner
back home
for people like him.
For people like me.
Come, hold my hand, he said
and don't let go
or we'll fall off the edge.
He vanished before the slow songs.

Before leaving

some of them seeded coded words
under sunflowers   milk thistle and jasmine.
Others submerged theirs   in paddy fields
or buried them
below nailed-muted floorboards   in dust.

These words were sacred
slipped from one tongue to another.

When the people arrived
somewhere safer   to new homes of straw
it took a lifetime to embrace
another language.   To learn
how to shout their own names.

Years later   some dared dream
of the words they had planted   imagining
a tangle of voices   strengthened by change
in season and soil.

Voices   stirring in apple orchards
palm groves   or sweetening acres of yam.
Voices pushing through clay   concrete
and bone.   Desire   lifting city smog
rising cautiously   like half-forgotten songs.

Prayer for The Fabulous Ones

Hail Big Maries, full of gin,
The Love is with thee.
Blessed art thou amongst drag queens,
and blessed is the fruit on thy headpiece. Jesus,
    that is the biggest drunkest Mary I've ever seen.
Holler-at-the-moon – you wigslip Mothers
    of Stonewall, Pride,
    of Russian queer rights activist,
    Yelena Grigoryeva, murdered
    after her address appeared online
    on a 'hit list', of Alireza Fazeli Monfared, 20,
    beheaded in Iran by members of his own family.
    Alireza loved lipsyncing and making TikToks.
    Remember Daniel Aston, Kelly Loving,
    Ashely Paugh, Derek Rump,
    Raymond Green Vance, shot dead
    at Club Q, Colorado Springs.
    Remember Brianna Ghey
    from Warrington – she was 16,
    the year of our Lord 2023.
Raise a pint to absent friends, Big Maries.
    Praise the lost, loved, living.
And forgive this poem's directness and sincerity.
Sashay for us, shade those
    who sing against us.
Now and at the hour of last orders.
                     Chin-chin.

The Rochdale Canal

When I find myself slipping, I hold on
and remember what the canal taught me:
No journey is a straight line.
The last time we walked here together,

I reminded you that not long ago this waterway
cut a dark scar through the Pennines, from Manchester
to Sowerby Bridge. Its future slippery, almost sunk.
But look at it now, you said. Look at the colours.

On a picnic bench by The Stubbing Wharf, you slipped
breaded scampi from your plate to mine. You always
ordered too much when eating out, loved to share
your good luck with family. I remember your smile.

I told you how horses hauled the cargo-heavy boats
back in the 1800s. How a wise farrier adapted the U
of a horseshoe with spiked nails to grip the towpath's wet stone.
Steady now. I remember you

smiling at that first slip of water over wood at Lock 11.
It can take an eternity to fill a void. Look at the ferns thriving
deep in the chamber wall, how they hold firm,
soft fingers outstretched, drowned, until the flood recedes

and the sun revives them. I remember your love
for these painted narrowboats, the way they garland
the canal bank like festival lanterns. Listen
to the jackdaws, slipping and tumbling above

the old mill chimney, their laughter echoing
in its throat. But where is our kingfisher?
She must be close, waiting to slip from a willow tree,
to swoop and sip her bright blue reflection.

crazydream i

he drops   to shattered knees   scrubs
    monochromatic tiles   the widening crack
sucks dry   a last tear of
                                    bleach

from the blue nozzle   whetting duster
with thin spittle   he flips-to-life a laptop
exposing filth   *rub-a-dub-dub*

buttons pressed too hard
whistling *The Archers*   he slips a wet wipe
    from the re-sealable hole   applies to

incisors   canines
                                    molars
squeak-squeak   scrapes bad words
from his tongue   with Nana's antler-handled

paper knife   *mustn't sleep*   *mustn't sleep*
he jolts himself   sands down
fingernails   & prints   to glassy veneers

some algorithms work better than others
    but hydrochloric acid dissolves   build-up

at the first lick   of sun-rise
                                    exit
the shed   turkey naked

dumps his broken memory   in the big skip
on Mrs Neighbour's driveway   activates
snooze-mode
   lies frost-framed   ice-bitten   silently emptying

and in the park beyond the dual carriageway
        blackthorn flares   immaculate white

crazydream ii

and after that I turned into a jay
        sloughing   mole pelt
              when the puffball blew
 its dark magic
        against my tongue

         my screams shook trees naked
        and the red moon rose
                  through me
      like fever   cobalt wings bared
      I was swept up
by a leaf blizzard to the peaks of

       a familiar terraced street
      chimney   by chimney
        I offered a lone blood feather
 to each hearth
      each home

       some pinned these keepsakes
     to their breasts
                some let them burn
     others buried theirs under peat
    and prayed
for a song thrush to grow

  my mother clutched hers   became Kestrel
       and flew high above the village   she let go
        then circled away
             quill drifting down
 to the reservoir's
      frozen mirror

tormentil +

cheek by soil
each bloom is a miniature masterpiece
four petals in perfect symmetry

north

west   east

south

so why do I feel lost
when a thousand compasses
guide the way?

The wave

I can hear the murmur of beachcombers,
the midnight surf sighing

over past lives. We walk the shoreline
in silence, remembering

what the ocean washed up just a week ago,
forgetting the moon tide until we're knee-deep.

You can choose to step into a body or over it.
Our hands find each other and I pull you free

of the water. We haul each other onto dry land,
cling like crabs to the pebble beach,

listen to the waves calling us back.
I give thanks to Mary, Patron Saint of the Sea.

When I turn to thank you,
I'm dazzled by the steady beam of a lighthouse.

Morning swim, 1979

Treading river in the soft mist
of a summer shower

I watch as a water vole
feasts on horsetail.

It snaps each stem in two
and slides both pieces

between its whiskers.
It does this again and again

ripple
    after
       ripple
    after
ripple.

Those eyes – two drops
of black rain – never leave mine

and for a moment
the boy in me

wants a stone to throw
to show who is king

of the great River Dane.
But the itch slips away

thrashes downstream
with the roach, bream, perch, grayling.

Water brought me to you
and it will sweep me away

On the A646
            under a drizzle-peppered sky
                        a man spits rage at a pair of domestic geese
            coddling a traffic cone.
                        At home, his wife rubs new potatoes,
    rinses away flakes of thin skin, over-salts a bubbling pan.
Next day, husband
                        loses his job and she takes the brakes off
            a lucrative career in
        industrial dehumidifiers. Key responsibility: being strapped
            to a desk near a vending machine that rattles
        like a hungover friend making tea.
                        She misses the squeaks and trills of her baby
                        but finds distraction
                                    in the grunts of complaint
    colleagues slop at her feet. In the shadow of a potted palm,
    the water cooler hums like a bored person. Back at the house,
the washing machine screeches
    as it nears the end of each cycle.
                        One night, husband's headphones
                        clatter to the herringbone floor. She asks
                        if he's awake. He purrs
                                    like a tiny motor.
        Perhaps, she thinks, he lives permanently behind glass
            like those trilby-topped men
                in his lopsided Hopper poster, praying for answers
                in the stains of a coffee mug.

Next morning, she swerves hard
to avoid a mute swan squatting on tarmac.
Unmoved, the bird stares sideways at the canal. A hiss
from the radio makes the woman suddenly tearful.
Swallowing sobs, she thinks of her baby, 78% spring water,
husband, 60% lake water, the dryness of machines,
how water can breach machinery,
how sphagnum moss holds twenty times
its mass in captive water. Leaving work early that day,
she stoops to listen to her daughter's babbling –
a peat-dyed valley stream,
frothy with every sound
in every language of the world.
When her baby falls asleep,
she lifts the child's soft-shelled mouth to her ear,
hears the ocean's
first word.

Silverfish

We live among you
but you don't see us.

We exist
in crawlspaces,

damp places,
cracks in walls.

We're waiting
for the night

when you wake at three,
stumble to the bathroom

to take inventory
of soaps, floss, shower gels.

With the lid down,
you'll sit and question

how you arrived here
and is it enough.

That's when we'll rise
between the floorboards

you're staring at.
See how we glisten

like drops
from a secret ocean.

But where do you really come from?

Philippines	31%
Japan	14%
Senegal	10%
China	8%
Vietnam	8%
Mozambique	7%
Mali	5%
Melanesia	2%
Cameroon, Congo & Southern Bantu Peoples	3%
Southern & Eastern India	2%
Northern & Western India	2%
Dai	2%
Korea & Northern China	1%
Eastern Europe & Russia	1%
European Jewish	1%
Ireland & Scotland	1%
Italy	<1%
Eastern Bantu Peoples	<1%

Rebirth

The day after you died,
you came back as a number.
One of 784.
The day after you died,
we rescued a new-born fawn
on the private lane to Nutclough.
The day after you died, Mum
and the next day and the next,
I catch your colours
in every living thing.
A red-tailed bumble bee
bending a Welsh poppy.
The robin eggs – glossy pearls
in their moss-padded nest.
Today, a moth judders
from the sock drawer, dusts my palm.
I open a window and blow.
Then I picture the mallards
flying low above your head
four summers ago. How you
pointed then cried,
'I love duck!' – the dropped
's' intentional for once.
On that delicious day,
I imagined a honking flock
of winged kitchen utensils
in hot pursuit of a flattened fowl.
Colanders. Cleavers. Chopping boards.
Your glinting favourite wok.

According to official reports, 784 people died in
England's hospitals from Covid-19 on April 18, 2020.

Cotton-grass, late spring

When tiredness drums,
lie down softly and
sift white clouds

through worn fingers,
the moss-plumped rock
your pillow.

Beyond the ridge,
traffic rasp rises and falls –
a giant's breath

at your neck.
Let the earth-herb scent
of heather, pre-bloom

sail and settle.
Cotton-sprawled and lulled
by curlew song

like a new-born
adrift in
mother-rhythm.

Turn away from
the forest with no trees,
those shadows in the walls.

Out of nowhere

two Chinooks
crack the sheen of summer.
Has the river broken its banks?
Are the moors kindling?
Is someone lost on the crags?
Two black dragonflies,
they skim the liquid valley,
dark blades slicing silence.
Echoes in a dream. A distant
door handle's rattle-clack.
Let me out. Let me out. Let me out.

Mouse-ear Hawkweed

'The herb bruised and bound to any cut or
wound doth quickly close the lips thereof.'
 – Nicholas Culpeper

Skirting the gravel pits of Dungeness –
a creeping yellow-headed plant
that isn't tormentil.
Close-up, its blooms are larger, blowsier,
more like small dandelions.
Yet this too is known for healing wounds.
What is it about tiny yellow flowers?
The way they scatter through spring grass,
a thin gauze of lemon magic. If only
there were enough of them to swathe
the earth. To *close the lips*. To hush
the hushed scream. But no –
I think instead of a woman's lips
pressed against a child's red-raw shin.
The sharpness of that pebble beach.
Hythe, 1970. I'm there, there, there.

Hairspray

It smelled like cheap wet paint
and pear drops. Got stuck
at the back of my throat. Vinyl
nails lacquered red. Ella spinning
on the turntable. Vermouth.
Brand new tights. Cleopatra
eyeliner. Zips, buckles, spritzer.
Two ropes of freshwater pearls.
Two lipsticks snapped shut
in a beige suede clutch. One boy
hovers by the dressing table.
Immoveable as your piled-high locks
with clip-on curls. Won't budge.

Falling galaxies

It's raining stars over the high moor,
the black sky flecked with slow cinders

coughed from the lungs of a great fire.
All week when we climb the hill at dusk

the spectacle materialises undimmed,
a kind of quiet obliteration. Some say

we come from stars and when we die
become them. I catch myself

glowing for the first time in months
when the moonface of a barn owl

appears above us by the old dye works.
A swirl of silver then she's gone.

From nowhere, a voice within me
blesses your name with the breath

of my childhood god. And for a few seconds
my words whiten the cold night air

like chalk on a blackboard. Like a question.

Vanishing act

Today I learnt a school friend died
suddenly last spring. Watkins –
terrible twosome they called us.
Hey, he asked me once, *do you want 50p?*
As I reached for the cash, his hand closed
as if he had something
not meant for the likes of me.
I prised open his fingers, one by one,
to reveal the coin had vanished.

Years later, at a friend's eighteenth,
Watkins said I was disgusting
for being queer. And… *poof!* …
just like that
                    I made him disappear.

The wood warbler's song

It's unmistakable,
a thin coin spinning on a plate.

The sound springs from nowhere
then somewhere over there.

Tangling itself round a thorn,
rising sharply through rusted bracken.

I pause until the high-pitched trill
stutters to a halt.

Heads
or tails?

It could go either way, the ICU doctor
warned us last night. And now I wonder

what news of you waits for me
down there in the valley

where my *no signal* phone
will chirp back to life in my hand.

hymnal

& the rock sang
why do you wait
for the sun

look how the wind
carves a bowl
into my body

look how the rain
fills the bowl
with fresh water

listen how the skylark
invites you
to ease your thirst

before the sun
reaches
across distant cities

flickering
with tiny yellow windows
& drinks the bowl dry

come
    kneel
cup your hands

Notes and Acknowledgements

Scrimshander: This poem was inspired by a Long-finned Pilot Whale skeleton on display at Leeds City Museum.

Nomi: Klaus Nomi was a German countertenor who came to prominence in New York's post-punk art scene. He died in 1983, aged 39, as a result of complications from AIDS.

Thanks to the editors of the following journals and anthologies in which some of these poems (including earlier versions and reprints) were published: *After Sylvia* (Nine Arches Press), *Bad Lilies, Butcher's Dog, Creative Writing: a Workbook with Readings* (Routledge), *Mapping the Future: The Complete Works Poets* (Bloodaxe Books), *Poetry Birmingham Literary Journal, Poetry London, Seconds: A Poetry Anthology from Rhubarb at the Triangle* (Ings Poetry), *Shadowtrain, The Dark Horse, The Poetry Review, The Rialto, tree – stone – sky – stream* (University of Macau and Malmö University), *Under the Radar, WHERE ELSE: An International Poetry Anthology* (Verve Poetry Press), *Yorkshire Times.*

Tormentil won a Royal Society of Literature 'Literature Matters' award while in progress. I am grateful to the RSL for their support which arrived at a crucial time in the collection's development.

I was honoured to be appointed Writer in Residence of the Brontë Parsonage Museum for 2023-24. Several poems in this collection were written or fine-tuned during the first half of the residency, and inspired by its 'Year of the Wild' theme and Haworth Moor.

The following organisations generously commissioned and published work that, in some form, also appears in this collection: The Poetry Society, Canal & River Trust, West Yorkshire Queer Stories, Sheffield Hallam University (*Matter* anthology).

A very early version of 'Lady Luck' won first prize in the PENfro Poetry Competition. 'Whose Story?' was a finalist in Manchester Writing School's Quiet Man Dave Prize.

Many poets offered invaluable feedback on a number of the poems, including Martin Kratz, Michael Conley, and members of Nine Lives Poets. Respect and appreciation to Carola Luther, Zaffar Kunial and Kim Moore for their generous testimonials.

Thanks to Jane Commane at Nine Arches Press for her skill, wisdom and guidance, and to Nine Arches' Angela Hicken.

Gratitude and love to Nigel for his continued patience.